GOD
in Unexpected Places

GOD
in Unexpected Places

□□□

Ira E. Williams, Jr.

ABINGDON PRESS   Nashville • New York

GOD IN UNEXPECTED PLACES

Copyright © 1974 by Abingdon Press

Library of Congress Cataloging in Publication Data

WILLIAMS, IRA E. 1926-   God in unexpected places. 1.
Christian life—1906-   I. Title.
BV4501.2.W542   248'.4   73-15522

ISBN 0-687-15122-8

Scripture quotations are from the Revised Standard
Version of the Bible, copyrighted 1946, 1952, 1971
by the Division of Christian Education, National Council of Churches, and are used by permission.

MANUFACTURED BY THE PARTHENON PRESS AT
NASHVILLE, TENNESSEE, UNITED STATES OF AMERICA

To Marilyn,

Who has brought to my life

Love and Joy and Beauty,

With just the right touch of

Wit to dethrone a king-sized ego,

Charm to restore it again,

And the intuition to know when.

A Foreword

A weary man fled across the plains of Canaan. He had deceived his father and betrayed his brother. All that once was sacred to him had been cheapened by his greed. When night came, he had no shelter from the cold and no pillow but a stone. At last he fell into a restless sleep and dreamed. When morning came, he woke to a haunting realization. The words of Jacob echo down the centuries: "Surely the Lord is in this place; and I did not know it."

This discovery of a lonely man is at the heart of the way God works. All of life is touched by his Spirit, yet he often makes himself known in a way we would least expect. His Word of Love in Christ was revealed in a stable, on a lakeshore, at a dinner party, on a street corner, from a hanging tree. Still God reveals his Word of Truth in unexpected places. Making this insight clear is the task of every pastor.

For twelve years, the people of First United Methodist Church in Albuquerque, New Mexico, have encouraged me to seek creative ways of getting across that message through the pastor's columns in our church paper. The following selections from those columns offer a thought for each week of the Christian year, making allowance for special days and a variance in the length of Epiphany and Pentecost. If this little book finds a welcome in your hands, the faith and prayers of a greathearted congregation will not have been in vain.

Words of gratitude are due Mrs. Ruth Cook, who edits the church paper; my wife, Marilyn, who typed the manuscript; our children, Mary, Jeanie, Shelley, and Wesley, who have shared with us the discovery of God in unexpected places; and my parents, from whom I first learned the wonder of his Presence.

Contents

CONTENTS

Kingdomtide

Advent

□□

*The season of expectation that recalls
the coming of God's Love into the
world through Jesus.*

Come, Lord Jesus

Come, infant Jesus, come! It's been so long since anyone made us stop and think what all our callous schemes do to the babies of the world.

Come, boy Jesus, come! It's been so long since anyone noticed that the questions of a twelve-year-old might be important.

Come, carpenter Jesus, come! It's been so long since anybody dared to believe God might be standing at a workbench as surely as in a church.

Come, teacher Jesus, come! It's been so long since most of us dared to think we still have something to learn—we're too busy talking to listen.

Come, friend Jesus, come! It's been so long that we've used our friends for stepping-stones to success, we've forgotten how to care for one another.

Come, physician Jesus, come! It's been so long that our bitter words and spiteful deeds have split us apart—we need to be made whole again.

Come, crucified Jesus, come! It's been so long that we've excused our sins, we need someone who will make us see what hate and prejudice do when they have run full course.

Come, living Christ Spirit, come! Bring the powers of holy Love to roll away the stone from the joyless tombs in which we've trapped ourselves.

And he said, "Have I been with you so long, and yet you do not know me? . . . . *I am with you always!*"

Do You Hear What I Hear?

It's a beautiful story they tell at Christmastime—all about a mother and baby, the shepherds who heard an angel's song at midnight, wise men bringing gifts.

But do we have the gift of God to hear the rest of the story? Do you hear the message the picture on the Christmas cards is all about?

Listen with me!

"You shall call his name Jesus, for he will save his people from their sins."

And Bill Smith said, "That's right! That *is* in the Bible story. It's quite a message for junkies and thieves and fallen women—for God to send a Son to save them from their sins."

But a still, small Voice said, "Friend, those aren't the only people who need a savior! What about *your* sins?"

16

The man was puzzled and he said, "What sins, Lord?"

The Voice answered, "The way you spend your money, the way you feel about Blacks and Chicanos, the way you talk to your employees, the way you neglect your family's spiritual needs, the way you lose your temper . . ."

And the man was thoughtful for a moment as he said, "I'm not sure I want to be saved from that kind of sin! "

You listen to the Christmas story, too! Do you hear what I hear?

Christmas Is Coming

Christmas is coming—the birthday of Christ the King!
I know it is—there are all the signs in the air:
 Only last night I heard the TV ad man telling me:
 "Do your Christmas buying now. Avoid all the con-
 fusion of the last-minute rush. Remember, there are
 only fifteen more shopping days until Christmas!"
Christ! Is this why you were born?

Christmas is coming—the birthday of Christ the King!
I know it is—there are all the signs in the air:
 Only yesterday I saw the display in a window of the

17

package store: "Raise the glass of good cheer this holiday season. Buy a fifth for yourself, and don't forget this beautifully wrapped bottle to bring Christmas joy to your friends."
Christ! Is this why you were born?

Christmas is coming—the birthday of Christ the King!
I know it is—there are all the signs in the air:
    This week I heard the movie singer telling everybody about the fellow in the big red suit wearing the long white whiskers. He was singing, "May Santa fill your hearts with love this Christmas . . ."
Christ! Is this why you were born?

Christmas is coming—the birthday of Christ the King!
I know it is—there are all the signs in the air:
    I happened to overhear a couple of late shoppers: "We got a present from the Smiths last year; guess we'll have to find one for them this year. But thank God the Williamses forgot us; that's one less thing to buy. He had the most horrid taste in gifts anyhow."
Christ! Is this why you were born?

Christmas is coming—the birthday of Christ the King!
I know it is—there are all the signs in the air:
    I heard a group of little children singing their hearts out in Sunday school: "Silent night, holy night, all is calm, all is bright." And I said:
Christ! This is why you were born! You were born for them!

And he answered me in the strangest way:

18

"Yes, this is why I was born! I was born for them. But don't forget—I was born and died for the others, too: The TV ad-man, the liquor dealer, the movie singer, the late shoppers . . .
You tell them that!"

All the World Loves a Baby

Last night I sat for a moment before the manger scene in our home. It is a miniature of the ones who were gathered together on that first holy night. There are beautifully carved figures of the shepherds and Mary and Joseph. The craftsman so worked with the child in the manger that the face of the infant Jesus is touched with the beauty of innocence that makes us love all babies.

I lifted the child from the manger scene and held the tiny figure in my hands. The Christ of God came into the world as a baby—a fragile, cuddly baby boy that a mother loved, and shepherds adored and even the serving girl at the inn must have smiled to see. No wonder we are touched with joy and love on Christmas Eve, as we sing of the holy Child, and the Love that is there, even in a shabby cattle stall.

But babies have a way of growing up!
And one day the man Christ Jesus stood before

people like you and me. And he showed them that:

Love sometimes has to condemn our selfishness.

Love sometimes has to judge our hating.

Love sometimes has to break our hearts.

Love sometimes has to destroy our prejudice.

Love sometimes has to make us do good to our enemies.

Love sometimes has to help people who won't love us back.

Many who had loved the baby Jesus hated the man Christ Jesus, for he showed them something about themselves they didn't want to admit was true.

It was sad that they refused to hear the rest of the message—his Father was their Father too, and would help them live as the children of God.

Almost two thousand years have come and gone. And still men love the baby Jesus, and reject the Truth of the man Christ Jesus. But that doesn't seem to weary God. His Love continues to be born again each year in the unworthy mangers of our human hearts.

Christmastide

□□□

The season of celebration that the Word became flesh and dwelt among us.

When Christ Was Born

When Christ was born—
Wise men came from the East looking for a king and bringing costly treasures to gain favor from one who would sit on an earthly throne.

They found instead a peasant woman hovering over a baby wrapped in rags, and were moved to share their wealth with the homeless and shivering family.

When Christ was born—
The zealots of the Jewish underground were looking for a leader with courage enough to drive the Roman army from their land.

They found instead a man who made them put away their swords and face the wrath of their enemies with no weapons but divine love and goodwill.

When Christ was born—
The Pharisees were looking for a messiah who would congratulate them for being such religious men.

They found instead a man whose look pierced the veneer of their bigotry and laid bare their empty souls.

When Christ was born—
The beggars in Jerusalem were looking for a comrade who would sympathize with their resentment and help them soak the filthy rich.

They found instead a carpenter who made them stand on their feet with dignity and pride as they joined him in the tasks he had for them to do.

When Christ was born—
The good people of Jerusalem were looking for a comforter to assure them that the sick and the poor at their gates had pretty well gotten what they deserved.

They found instead a physician who taught them to heal the sick and have compassion for the poor.

When Christ was born—
He denied men what they asked for, and gave them what they needed. If that happens to you, don't become bitter—accept it thankfully.

They Knelt at the Manger!

It wasn't an easy thing to do—what Mary did:
  Hearing her friends whisper that she had to get married . . .

Making the long ride to Bethlehem on the back of a
clumsy donkey . . .
Birthing her firstborn in a cow shed to be laid on
the straw.
But she did it—and thanked God for the privilege!

It wasn't an easy thing to do—what Joseph did:
Believing in the innocence of the pregnant girl he
was engaged to marry . . .
Accepting the abuse from short-tempered innkeep-
ers in the little town . . .
Risking his life to take Mary and the baby to Egypt
in the face of Herod's anger.
But he did it—and thanked God for the privilege!

It wasn't an easy thing to do—what the wise men did:
Crossing the desert to Bethlehem with no guide
but a star and a prayer of faith . . .
Giving their costliest possessions with no hope of
receiving in return . . .
Accepting the disfavor of a hotheaded king rather
than betray an innocent family.
But they did it—and thanked God for the privilege!

It wasn't an easy thing to do—what you did:
Giving an afternoon each week to call at the nurs-
ing home . . .
Praying for that man who did you wrong, in the
presence of your children . . .
Taking those Cuban kids into your home while
their mother was in the hospital.

But you did it—and thanked God for the privilege!

In a way, *you* knelt at the manger, too!

Let Us Break Bread Together

In a sacred covenant with God, at the beginning of this New Year, I take in hand the bread and wine —and pause to remember:

That . . . He who can number the infinite stars
in their courses,
Knows ME too!
He who sees when even the feeblest
sparrow falls,
Knows ME too!
He who watches the waving in the
spring breeze
of even the lily in the fields,
Knows ME too!
But . . . The deceit in the life of Judas who
betrayed with a kiss,
Is in ME too!
The blindness of a mob that rejected and
taunted its Deliverer,
Is in ME too!
The fire of hate and selfish desire that
burned in the hearts of some Pharisees
Is in ME too!

CHRISTMASTIDE

Yet . . . The look in the eyes of Christ that
brought Peter to tears of repentance,
Is turned to ME too!
The finger that wrote in the sand bring-
ing life to an adulteress,
Writes for ME too!
The lips that spoke forgiveness for a
tortured thief on a cross,
Speak to ME too!

I am known and judged . . .
Yet forgiven!
O God, if it is so . . .
Then how can I not forgive as I kneel to receive
the symbols of him who came . . . for *me!*

Epiphany

□□

*The season of wonder that God
makes himself known to men in the
life of our world day by day.*

Tom Jones Looks at His World

Tom Jones sat at his desk and he said, "I think I will make a map of my world."

So he unfolded a map of the city and began marking the places that made up his little private world. He put a big circle on the page each time he called off the locations:

1. This is the place where I work.
2. This is the place where I keep my money.
3. This is the place where I get my hair cut.
4. This is the place where I go out to dinner.
5. This is the place where I buy my clothes.
6. This is the place where I service my car.
7. This is the place where I play golf.
8. This is the place where I go to my lodge.

Then he sat back and looked at the map of his world. Suddenly he remembered—something was missing. Isn't every good American supposed to have a religion? So Tom picked out a church to complete the map of his private world.

But one day something happened in church that Tom Jones had not made a place for in his little private world. On a never-to-be forgotten Sunday, he met his Master face to face.

After that, he went home and threw away his map, for he found that a man's world is not places on a map. A man's world is people. Whether it's worth living in the world depends on what you do and are, with people. Tom Jones discovered his new Master had some very important things to say on that subject!

What kind of private world do you think you have?

Still He Speaks!

A herder of sheep on the plains of Egypt sees a burning bush and hears the voice of God calling him to do an impossible job—

But he does it!

And today's man argues whether Moses really saw a miracle—because it is easier to defend or re-define the past than to answer the call of God for today.

A carpenter walks the streets of an ancient city, stops by a pool of water and tells a cripple to do an impossible thing—

But he does it!

And today's man argues whether Jesus really healed

the cripple—because it is easier to defend or re-define the past than to let Christ heal our crippled spirits
and set us free today to walk as the children of God.

A tentmaker travels along a mountain road and
hears a voice calling him to make an impossible
change—
But he does it!
And today's man argues whether Paul really heard
a voice—because it is easier to defend or re-define
the past than to answer the call of God to shed the
cloak of our own prejudice and misdirected zeal.

And what about you? I fear that I am too often
"today's man."

What Happened to God?

Suddenly I felt cold and alone in the world, and
wondered if there is a God who knows or cares anymore—or if there ever was!
I went to the observatory and put my eyes to the
giant telescope, and as I scanned the night skies I
found no trace of God.
I went up into the mountains and watched the
stream churning in little pools as it ran down over the
rocks. A cloud bank covered the sun and the whole

33

world turned cold, and the God I looked for in nature did not show his face.

I went to the church and sat in the pew, and looked at the cross on the altar and the faces in the windows. But the cross was only a lovely piece of handicraft to me, and the face in the window was stiff and un-moving. And the God whom I hoped to find there escaped me again.

And I said, "They are right, these men—God is dead."

I moved on down the street and passed the home of a man lonely and in trouble. A half-forgotten phrase kept intruding its way into my thoughts: "As you did it to one of the least of these my brethren, you did it unto me." For some reason I turned back to the home of the lonely man and shared his troubles.

Leaving his home, I looked up at the stars and sensed the mystery of the Divine.

I lifted my eyes to the hills and praised the Creator for the wonder of the world he had made.

I stepped into the church and thanked God for the Christ who became known to me through sharing the burdens of my brother.

It Doesn't Pay to Second-Guess God

It was a cold and cruel world the Christians of the first century had to face. They were huddled together in little house churches in the distant reaches of the Roman world, trying to make sense of their task as Christians. They became more discouraged each day with the crude and hardened life-style of their pagan neighbors.

So they recalled some words of Jesus about the end of time and decided the hour was close at hand. With a high sense of expectation they gave up on their present world and waited for the end . . . but it never came. And finally, they had to settle down and put their minds and hearts and hands to making the best they could of the world God had given them.

And sure enough, some good things happened.

In some of the bleakest years of the Middle Ages Christian men despaired of their world. It was cruel and vulgar, and civilization was at so low an ebb they were sure the words of ancient prophecy were about to be fulfilled for the end of time.

So, in 1492 a group of church leaders met to make their preparations for the end of the world . . . but it never came. Instead, it was the dawning of a new day for mankind as a few men put their minds and hearts and hands to making the best they could of the world God had given them.

And sure enough, some good things happened.

There are many things about our world that are unpleasant. We are reaping the blighted harvest of dishonor in high places. Our great energies in science and technology have created as many problems as they have benefits. The traffic in crime and drugs is so terrifying many of us do not sleep well at night.

It is no wonder "The Jesus People" have started prophesying the end of the world, and many Christians are ready to throw up their hands and give in to despair . . . but the world is not likely to end any time soon. So we may as well settle down and put our minds and hearts and hands to making the best we can of the world God has given us.

And sure enough, some good things will happen.

The Sights and Sounds of the City

Today I walked along the street, and I was struck by the sights and the sounds of the city. It was a screeching, cold, and heartless city. There was
the mad rush of the freeway traffic;
the scramble for bargains at a department store
    entrance;
the babble of voices arguing about little issues;
the clang of cash registers marking up the sacrifices
    offered to the gods of mammon;
the people like robots, so intent on their personal
    errands they never really saw the others passing
    by.

And I cried out, "O God, what a horrible way to

waste your years. Let me retreat to the hills and never walk these streets again."

And God said, "I will go with you, in the way you have walked."

So, once again I moved along the street, and I was struck by the sights and the sounds of the city. No longer was it a screeching, cold, and heartless city, for I found that

the freeway traffic was not a mass of cars, but a man and a woman and a child—people like me;

the scramble for bargains was not so mad as I thought when I remembered how my own wife stretched her grocery money to cover material for the girls' dresses at the bargain counter;

the babble of voices did not seem nearly so distracting when I was the one who did the talking;

the clang of cash registers was music to my ears when it rang up a purchase of the perfect gift I had found for my son;

and when I saw the nurse on her way to the hospital room, the officer stopping traffic to let a blind man cross the street, the banker helping a family plan for a house, I knew that at least some who passed by me were not just people like robots.

God did not need to say more to me as we walked along. For I knew that both countryside and city are only as cold and heartless and ugly as men like me make them.

What Is the Real Story?

Our world has a strange way of holding in the limelight men and women who have little business being there, and giving the impression to the man in the street that we are a nation of fools!

For instance: A rabble-rouser stands on a soapbox and works to incite the emotions of men: "Riot, baby, riot . . . burn, baby, burn." He is loud enough that his press coverage gives him credentials to speak for the man in the ghetto.

And yet: Scores of dedicated men in that same city are working to find humane solutions for the problems that have driven people of the ghetto to follow the rabble-rouser on the soapbox.

For instance: A woman whose chief talent for the theater is a bulging bosom tries to act and falls on her face. But after the lurid details of a few sordid affairs are featured in the slick magazines, she becomes a rising star in the film world, though she still can't act.

And yet: The theater in the twentieth century is still a healthy enterprise because thousands of people on campuses and little theaters across the country love to act and gladly follow the disciplines it takes to be a good performer.

For instance: A pompous buffoon presides over a meeting of men. Only a sequence of unbelievable circumstances could have made him their leader, but he basks in the glory of his authority.

And yet: The men who work under him are committed to so great a vision they ignore his arrogance and put their best talents to work for the greater good of their homes, churches, and communities.

What is the real story? The things that happen behind the scenes often measure a nation's greatness better than events and people who hit the headlines. This is one of the glories of the church—what a carpenter did in Nazareth was more important than what a king did in Jerusalem. In quiet, seemingly insignificant ways, God is at work building integrity in the lives of men who call him Lord.

Before We Turn Our Backs

The Men's Bible Class wasn't happy with the lesson treatment in their quarterly on Brotherhood Sunday. Finally, one of them summed it up, "These writers can say what they want, but I never saw a Jew that wouldn't make a fast buck if he got the chance."

And, remembering his own heritage, the Good Shepherd in the picture above them knew he wasn't wanted, hung his head, and left the room.

A cluster of teen-agers in a church youth meeting started snickering when a strange boy came into the room. One of the group who knew his carefully guarded secret had just blurted out, "I happen to know his old lady didn't get married till after he was born."

And, remembering the stories about his own mother, the Child in the manger scene above them knew he wasn't welcome, and faded from their sight.

The couple in the foyer saw a frail man walk through the door and recognized him as a parolee released from jail only a short time ago. The woman turned her back to him and said to her husband, "He'd better not go to our Sunday school class. I'm not about to sit in the room with a man that has a police record."

And remembering his own arrest and trial and sentencing, the Figure on the cross above the door knew he wasn't wanted and silently slipped away.

Before we turn our backs on any rejected member of the human family, it might be well to ask whether he has more in common with Jesus than we do.

God Comes

In such a casual way, we say, "God comes."

How can we take for granted so bold a claim! Try to imagine for a moment the supreme Intelligence who dreamed a world and set the stars on their courses. To say such a God cares about men almost seems like a blubbering arrogance. And yet, this is our faith.

But the wisdom of the Bible was never very logical.

Men were always so sure that God stood on the rim of space and looked down at humanity with little more than scorn or pity or an occasional act of benevolence. They were so sure—until they looked into the face of a child in a manger and dared to say, "God is with us."

Men were always so sure that God was like a king who enjoyed his power and dominated his subjects. They were so sure—until they looked in the face of a carpenter riding a jackass into a city and saw him make weak people strong.

Men were always so sure that God would want them to deal cruelly with all who were different from his favored worshipers. They were so sure—until they looked in the face of a man on a cross asking a Father God to forgive his tormentors.

Remembering these things—how do you think God would come to you?

Perspective

A lonely shepherd on a mountainside
   Led his sheep by the flowing streams
And thought how like to a caring God,
   Loving his creatures, sharing their dreams.
While I see a flock of sheep by a pool
And think lamb chops and cardigan wool.

An exile brooded by the river Chebar,
   As Babylon's trade throbbed wheel on wheel,
And dreamed of a God, in days of despair,
   Who turns men brave with a holy zeal.
While the wheels I see both near and far
Tempt me to buy a late-model car.

A carpenter spoke of lilies in a field
   To friends with whom he walked about,
And praised the beauty God provides
   That even weeds cannot choke out.
While I cross meadows constantly knocking
Spears of dried stubble caught in my stocking.

The judgment stands through the centuries—
A man is measured by what he sees!

Lent

□□

*The season of penitence and openness
to the judgment God must make on
us and our world.*

A Penance for Lent

Once there was a man who started taking short-cuts in his business. He was a contractor and had a chance at times to substitute inferior materials and workmanship and still get them by the inspector. He consoled himself with the argument that everybody's doing it.

As a penance, he decided to make up for it by giving the church an extra hundred dollars during Lent.

It never occurred to him that there are some things you can't make up for that way.

Once there was a woman who became upset because of something that was said by a member of the church. The more she thought about it the angrier she became. And so she began to talk about the other woman. She never bothered to challenge her adversary face to face, but her words were so vicious she finally drove the woman from the church in disgrace.

As a penance, she decided to form a prayer group in her home during Lent.

It never occurred to her that there are some things you can't make up for that way.

Once there was a teen-aged boy who took his girl friend out for a date. After a movie he insisted on parking for awhile on the mesa. The girl protested, but he assured her he only wanted to talk. Before long he had forced his attentions on her in a way that violated something sacred to the girl, and he bragged about it to his buddies the next day.

As a penance, he gave up cokes during Lent and bought Easter seals with the money he saved.

It never occurred to him that there are some things you can't make up for that way.

But Jesus said, "Leave your gift there before the altar and go; first be reconciled to your brother, and then come and offer your gift."

Where Do You Stand?

It was a moment of decision. The Rich Young Ruler had listened as Jesus lay before him the chance of a lifetime. He could become the thirteenth disciple. The great talent that made him a man of wealth at such an early age could mean much under the direction of the Master of men. He was ready to go, until Jesus demanded from him a spirit that was something his money couldn't buy. The Rich Young Ruler turned his back, and sadly walked away.

It was a moment of truth. Nicodemus, that great Jewish scholar, had listened to Jesus at a distance. He began to think this carpenter from Nazareth might be the leader his nation needed—a man like the prophet Amos, perhaps. He was ready to listen, until Jesus exposed the ignorance of the man in things that really mattered and made Nicodemus look at the emptiness of his own life. The Jewish scholar closed his mind and dismissed the words of Jesus as nonsense.

It was a moment of destiny. Jesus had listened to the call of God to live out the Father's Love in the world. The people responded when Love meant healing the sick, feeding the hungry, being kind to children; but when Love had to come as Judgment, the people weren't sure they wanted to listen anymore. Once again God called Jesus to decide whether he would live out the Father's Love, even if he had to die for the sake of the Truth about God and men. In that stark, lonely hour of decision, "he set his face to go to Jerusalem," whatever it cost.

Too often I fear that I stand with Nicodemus and the Rich Young Ruler . . . and so seldom with Jesus!

47

A Substitute?

A poor man stopped me on the street and looked into my soul with pleading eyes. I took a bill from my wallet and pushed it into his hand. With a certain contentment at having done my good deed for the day, I hurried on to the post office.

—And yet, while walking down the street, I remembered again the look in his eyes, and was haunted by the thought that he may have been more hungry for my friendship than my money.

A young neighbor boy came to the door and asked me to buy some Boy Scout candy. I abruptly dished out the price of two boxes, so his folks wouldn't think me a cheapskate, and slammed the door.

—And yet, in shuffling back to the den, I wondered what it might have done for the boy if I had shown a personal interest in him and his scouting projects.

My wife was feeling low one day when I stopped by the house to look for some papers. So I opened my billfold and shelled out enough for a new outfit to cheer her up, then hurried off before I became depressed myself.

—And yet, while driving away I kept wondering if what she really needed was not a new suit, but more of my time, and a way of caring for which money was no substitute.

Friend, do you ever let money become a substitute for caring?

Would You Dare?

Timothy Morgan was ambitious, and he didn't like the problems the government was causing in his determination to be a wealthy man. He read somewhere that Christianity was the foundation stone of American freedom and decided perhaps he should try it. He bowed his head, with a Bible in hand, and prayed, "God, show me the Christian answer to my problems."

Then he opened his Bible and found the words of Jesus, "Sell what you have, and give to the poor . . . and come, follow me."

And he closed the Bible, muttering, "That wasn't exactly the answer I was looking for!"

John Smith was having trouble with a man whom he instinctively disliked. He wondered what could be done to get this character out of his hair for good. A friend told him there was a "sure-fire" way to take care of your enemies. John jumped at the chance to settle the score with his tormentor. The friend took out a pocket New Testament and opened it for John to read.

There was a passage marked, "Love your enemies and pray for those who persecute you."

John handed back the Bible and walked away. "Some friend to pull a dumb trick like that."

Mary Johnson had been hurt because of something that was said at a church meeting. She couldn't understand why women who claimed to be Christian could talk that way to one another. So she decided, "If that's the way they are they can just have their old church, and to heck with it. I can worship God without the church."

Mary picked up her Bible and it happened to fall open at the place where Paul was writing to some disgusted members of the church at Ephesus, "Be kind to one another, tenderhearted, forgiving one another, as God in Christ forgave you."

Closing the book, she thought to herself, "The Bible isn't always comforting, is it?"

Would you dare to take some of *your* problems to Christ—for *his* answer?

When a Question Became an Answer

A man who had been lame for years lay on his pallet beside a pool of water. The Master of men was passing by and the crippled man looked up to the Christ with pleading eyes. Jesus asked him, "Do you want to be healed?"

And the lame man knew Jesus had seen the emptiness of his soul. In this moment he had to decide which was most precious to him: his self-pity and the attention smothered on him by a doting family—or the responsibility of new life as a man made whole.

A religious leader stood before the Master of men and asked a question of him as though he would put him to a test, "What shall I do to inherit eternal life?" Jesus answered by asking a question, "What is written in the law? How do you read?"

And the man knew Jesus had seen the emptiness of his soul. In this moment he had to admit that his claim to be in search of some new truth about God was only a way of evading his very evident obligations to God and man.

A woman caught in the act of adultery lay trembling in the dust of a city street. The Master of men stooped to write in the sand, and an angry mob of men who had judged her read the words in the sand: "Let him who is without sin among you be the first to throw a stone at her." The frightened harlot lifted her eyes to the Christ, and he asked, "Where are they? Has no one condemned you?"

And the woman knew Jesus had seen the emptiness of her soul. As the men who had condemned her dropped their stones and walked away with heads hung in shame, she could no longer justify her sins as no worse than the pride of the self-righteous ones in the city.

Two talented brothers stepped aside as their mother stood before the Master of men and asked that her sons be given places of honor in the leadership of the kingdom, because of their creative abilities. Jesus by-passed the ambitious mother to ask of the sheepish sons, "Are you able to drink the cup that I drink?"

And the two sons knew Jesus had seen the empti-ness of their souls. In that moment it became crystal clear that Christ was ushering in a new kind of king-dom where becoming a loving servant to suffering humanity would bestow on them a dignity as the sons of God that was its own reward.

What Bothers Me

I have to confess that I find the Bible embarrassing to me at times.

For instance: "Jesus was coming to Jerusalem. So they took branches of palm trees and went out to meet him, crying, 'Hosanna! Blessed is he who comes in the name of the Lord! . . .' And Jesus found a young ass and sat upon it."

That bothers me! The sight of Jesus coming to the big city on one of those stupid-looking animals robs him of the dignified image he ought to have!

Or is my problem something else—*that I am too*

proud to associate myself with any symbol of the lowly and despised of earth?

For instance: "Jesus entered the temple of God and drove out all who sold and bought in the temple, and he overturned the tables of the money-changers and the seats of those who sold pigeons. He said to them, 'It is written, "My house shall be called a house of prayer"; but you have made it a den of robbers!' "

That bothers me! It shows a side of Jesus I don't like. Those men had families to support. They were within the law. He didn't have to make a federal case of it. He could have gone through the proper channels without making a big scene.

Or is my problem something else—*that I don't want Jesus interfering with my own selfish systems that leave no place for God in my life?*

For instance: Jesus said, "Woe to you, scribes and Pharisees, hypocrites! For you tithe mint and dill and cummin, and have neglected the weightier matters of the law, justice and mercy and faith. . . . The tax collectors and the harlots go into the kingdom of God before you."

That bothers me! Jesus is supposed to be a symbol of kindness and gentleness, yet here he is talking to the most religious men in the church as if they were perverted crooks. He isn't true to his image, the way I see it.

Or is my problem something else—*that I had rather be the judge of what men live by than let Jesus judge me for my motives?*

Seven Days

Seven days—a week—such a little bit of time out of all the years that men have lived. But how much can take place in only seven days!

The whole drama of the life of man was once lived out in seven days. It was such a long time ago—and yet it could have been only yesterday.

There was a man coming into a city. Everybody was praising him. The world was beautiful in spring, and the hearts of men were as warm as the sun shining on the flowering almonds.

But the next day the innocence of Holy Love in the life of the man who rode into the city made the lives of the men of the city look ugly and shabby in his presence. The men of the city were ashamed—

but shame turned to remorse—
remorse turned to rationalization—
rationalization turned to selfishness—
selfishness turned to resentment—
resentment turned to bitterness—
bitterness turned to hate—
hate turned to violence.

There was a hanging tree outside the city, and on the sixth day, the man who rode into the city was nailed to the hanging tree. As the sun went down, they took him down and laid him in a tomb.

Only—someone had forgotten that Holy Love can't

stay closed up in a tomb. The next morning the man who rode into the city seven days before was back in the city again.

Across the centuries he comes riding back. He came to Albuquerque this morning!

Eastertide

□□□

The season of celebration that God gives victory over sin and death through Jesus Christ.

It Keeps on Coming

I wake up in the morning to the sound of a news-caster telling the atrocities of violence among the nations; my heart is torn to see on television the face of a young girl screaming in terror only seconds after the explosion of a dreaded napalm bomb; I am sick at my stomach to think of the innocent who bleed and die from the hit-and-run guerrilla raids; and I begin to question whether mankind even deserves to sur-vive—

except that Easter keeps on coming!

I read in the magazines of the things we have done for the sake of the dollar we worship: the little dead birds with the oily muck on their wings lie on the beaches; somebody's elderly father chokes to death in the polluted air of skies that once were clear; a small boy catches hepatitis from swimming in the once beautiful Potomac River which is now only a dirty sewer; and I am sure we will go ahead and damn ourselves to extinction—

except that Easter keeps on coming!

I look about me and see parents who never seem to care what their children do or where they are, then turn and blame the country's problems on the young; I see adults who turn over school buses that carry innocent children, and young people who do violence against innocent adults; I see some who demand unreasonable change in systems and others who defend unreasonable systems that must be changed; and I am sure there is no hope for any of us—
except that Easter keeps on coming!

I think of my personal struggles to put away bitterness toward those who overshadow me, then remember how little progress I make; I watch a good man die of cancer when I know that a better look at our spending priorities could have developed by now a cure for the frightening killer; I think of my church with its trials and agony as it seeks to reach those who have lost the Way, and as it works for a better world —yet so often fails at both; and I am sometimes ready even to give up on God—
except that Easter keeps on coming!

Easter Is Ended!

Easter is ended!
The last lovely anthem has been sung . . . the last sermon on the living presence of the Christ has been

spoken . . . the last little girl in a pretty bonnet cheering an angelic face has walked out the doors of the church . . . and the custodian of the building has just picked up the last scraps of paper that cluttered the empty sanctuary.

Easter is ended!

Or so I thought it was . . .

Until I saw a father stand by a small boy in a hospital bed, confident that God could be trusted with his dying son.

Until I saw a mother patiently give of herself to instill love and character into the heart of a daughter.

Until I saw a man who has broken the grip of one of the most vicious habits that can take hold of a person.

Until I saw a child give up a toy he cherished, because a sick friend had seen it and looked at it longingly.

Until I saw a teen-aged girl cheerfully take over the management of the household while her mother went to care for a neighbor in trouble.

And for so long as I see in the lives of others the love and understanding and sacrifice that God gave our world when Jesus came . . . then I shall know in the highest sense—

Easter is never ended!

I Was There—I Am Here

I stand before the mirror of the judgment of God and remember the words and the deeds of my life.

And I tremble because . . .

My ears have listened for fragments of filth to pass on about another man, just as ears once welcomed the words of slander in Pilate's courtyard.

My lips have betrayed something sacred in the life of another, as surely as lips that once cried out, "Crucify him!"

My feet have run to do dirty work, as surely as feet that once joined with a mob surging through the streets of Jerusalem.

My hands have driven nails into the heart of another, as surely as hands that once nailed a body to crossed slabs of wood on a hill called Calvary.

And I hate the reflection in the mirror of God's judgment—for I was there when they crucified my Lord.

Then suddenly the mirror becomes an open door —and through the open door I see the sons of men suffering as the Son of Man once suffered.

And so I dedicate . . .

My ears to hear the lonely cries of those caught up in the traps of their own making, as ears that once heard the cry of a lonely man in a sycamore tree.

My lips to speak words of comfort and understanding to the sorrowing and condemned, as lips that once spoke forgiveness to a dying thief.

My feet to run errands of love and mercy for the children of my Father, as feet that once turned aside to show compassion for the fevered daughter of an enemy of Israel.

My hands to lift up the burdens of those oppressed by their brothers' sins, as hands that once ministered to a helpless stranger on the road to Jericho.

And as I walk through the open door—I begin to know for the first time what Easter is all about.

Thoughts for Eastertide

Spring came early this year to Albuquerque.

The grass turned green in winter; the peach limbs blossomed; apricots formed on the trees, and the flowers broke forth in beauty along the hills, in the valleys and on a thousand lawns.

Then, last night the winds blew in from the North. A mass of cold air moved over the city. The snow covered our mountains, and a deep freeze came down on the beauty of the good earth.

Now the flowers are blighted with the cold, and there will not be fruit on our trees at harvesttime.

But there will be another spring, when the earth will again be clothed in beauty. The storm and the killing freeze will not come, the trees will be filled with good fruit at harvesttime, and our hearts will be glad.

There are blighted springs in the lives of men.
In the lives of men there is also the promise that there will be another spring!

A Litany for Family Week

Mama's at her weekly bridge club,
Mama's at the council of the PTA,
Mama's secretary for the Precinct Meeting,
Mama's out working for the Junior Service League—
    Johnnie's sitting in the den alone,
    Wondering when Mama's coming home.

Papa's at the golf course,
Papa's at a cocktail party,
Papa's high man on the bowling team,
Papa's out working on the Rotary Youth Committee—
    Johnnie's walking the streets alone,
    Wondering when Papa's coming home.

Johnnie's at a love-in,
Johnnie's at a pot party,

Johnnie's found the dream world of LSD,
Johnnie's out with all the gang raising hell tonight—
    Mama and Papa sit in the den alone,
    Wondering when Johnnie's coming home.

A Woman Remembers

The frail woman fell across an ancient bed and wept bitter tears for her son. He was only thirty-three —so very young to die.

This was not the future she had dreamed for her firstborn that night she gave him birth in a strange little town on a winter's night.

How much she had loved him. He was so thoughtful, so helpful with the younger children. She never would forget his face that day he folded up his carpenter's apron, took one last look around the shop and left her standing in the doorway.

And he had such a way with people—a dark room seemed to light up when he walked in. But now he was gone.

His dying seemed so senseless. If only the handful of rulers who decided his destiny could have really seen people the way he saw them—with his love for everybody—this wouldn't have had to happen.

But the bitterest part of all was that so many of those he died for didn't seem to care.

"Surely it's only a dream," she cried. "That's it—a bad dream."

But no, she knew better. She turned and picked up the telegram: "We regret to inform you . . . your son . . . killed in action . . ." The words all ran together through her tears.

It wasn't a dream!

O please, dear Christian friend—for her sake, and for the sake of all the mothers of the world—work and pray for peace!

It Doesn't Make Sense!

Last night I picked up a copy of the Bible and thumbed through it. I was struck by certain passages that never before had come across with such forcefulness.

There was that night when the shepherds walked in from the hills to Bethlehem. They gathered around a baby wrapped in rags and laid in the feed trough of a foul-smelling stable. And they were bubbling over with excitement that this was "good news of great joy."

It just doesn't make sense!

Another chapter in the Bible tells of a day when the people turned their backs on Jesus. There were friends aplenty when he was healing the sick and feeding the hungry, but he had just laid out the tough responsibilities demanded of anyone who would follow him. The crowd thinned out in seconds, and he was left with only a handful of true friends. In that moment Jesus spoke one of his most beautiful prayers of thanksgiving.

It just doesn't make sense!

The book of Acts talks about the disciples after Jesus was gone. He had been executed on a hanging tree and judged a criminal by the leaders of the city. The authorities used every means possible to dishonor his memory and to shame his followers. But the friends of Jesus came together and talked about the hanging tree as the symbol of a Love that could bless all humanity, and when they were thrown in jail for making such wild statements, they sang glad songs of joy from their prison cells.

It just doesn't make sense!

Unless, friend, they knew something that you and I may not know!

The Warm Heart

The message of John Wesley most often quoted is the simple phrase, "I felt my heart strangely warmed."

The problem is that most of us never move to the very next words of Wesley, without which the first have little meaning: "I felt I did trust in Christ, Christ alone, for my salvation; and an assurance was given me that He had taken away my sins, even mine, and saved me from the law of sin and death. I began to pray with all my might for those who had in a more especial manner despitefully used me and persecuted me."

The warm heart is a wonderful part of our Christian heritage. But without the sense of trust in God who speaks through Christ as the one great commitment of our lives—and the change in attitude that follows such a commitment—the warm heart becomes nothing more than a sentimental feeling we have when everything is going the way we want it to.

For example: Ted Brown can sing "Blessed assurance, Jesus is mine" with a glow on his face that makes you feel here's one guy who really enjoys his religion. But he wasn't civil to anybody for weeks after the last election when his candidates went down to defeat. *Faith in Christ alone?*

For example: Sally Smith always talks about working for "my Lord" and mentions without embarrassment how much she enjoys doing Jesus' work. But every time she comes around, she fills my ear with dirt about some church member, as though I must believe she is the only real Christian in the church. *Faith in Christ alone?*

For example: Ned Wilson has been a Christian since he was gloriously converted at the age of twenty, and you can tell by the look on his face that he puts his whole heart into the service on Sunday morning. But when he found how the Board voted to use an estate someone left the church, he turned bitter because he thought it should be used another way. He hasn't forgiven some of the men yet! *Faith in Christ alone?*

For example: There's not anyone who can offer a prayer like Molly Pitcher—warm and wonderful. A person can't help wishing he felt his religion the way she does. But Molly goes to pieces every time she has to shake hands with a Negro, and she fidgets until she can reach the closest lavatory to wash her hands. *Faith in Christ alone?*

For example: Ira Williams knelt to pray one night with an open Bible in his hand and as he prayed, his "heart was strangely warmed." But he keeps on judging people when Jesus said, "Judge not, that you be not judged." *Faith in Christ alone?*

Still God makes it possible for all of us not only to have our hearts strangely warmed but also to trust in Christ alone for our salvation. Then it is that nothing can shake us, and we do not run down others to build up ourselves.

Pentecost

□□□

The season of the church and its witness that the Spirit of God is at work in the fellowship of believers.

Pentecost!

The hucksters haven't yet learned a way to "make a good thing" of Pentecost as they do with Christmas and Easter, so we often ignore it. But it is one of the great days of our Christian faith—the birthday of the church.

It must have been a moving experience to be there that day. Luke tells us a hundred twenty people were gathered in the upper room where it happened. Think of it—all the glory of the church began with only a hundred twenty people, touched by a new Spirit.

Do you know why God was able to work through those one hundred twenty people? It was because of some things that *didn't* happen:

Bartholomew *didn't* turn aside to Philip and say: "I don't like the idea of a little clique running the church."

Mary *didn't* blurt out to Elizabeth: "I can't stand to hear Peter preach! He's always talking about what he and Jesus did as if there weren't any other disciples."

James *didn't* jut out his jaw and shout: "What do you

mean 'get a better place to meet'? If this room was good enough for Jesus, it's good enough for me!"

Thomas *didn't* get his dander up and say: "Well, if they're going to let in a couple of pious old frauds like Ananias and Sapphira, count me out."

Clopas *didn't* whisper under his breath to Salome: "Why did they make a mousy little runt like Andrew chairman of the Board?"

Martha *didn't* drop the words of scorn to Rachel: "Would you believe Mary Magdalene for President of the Ladies' Aid?"

Joseph Barsabas *didn't* complain: "They can have their old church—giving Judas' place to Mathias!"

But Luke tells us, "With one accord they devoted themselves to prayer."

It must be hard for a church to go bad when all the members honestly pray for one another. And so, I prayed, "God, I'd like to see Pentecost happen all over again, right here in my church!"

And God said, "Be careful how you pray! *It really can happen again!* Would you be ready for what follows?"

Not Even a Chance

I was visiting with a college freshman not long ago. He is a sharp kid, but a little confused by the university complex and a world where so many things are a mixture of good and evil now that he must make all his own decisions. He is much awed by the sophistication of his student world and would not want his friends to know about our conversation, although he has a suspicion some of them are whistling in the dark too.

I asked about his home life before he went to college. The parents were church members, but only attended at Easter. They felt religion had been shoved down their throats as children and were determined that was one indignity their son would not have to suffer. Their efforts were most successful, as I soon discovered:

He said he didn't believe in God—but he had never learned enough about Christianity to know what kind of God he didn't believe in!

He agreed with a professor of his that prayer is only wishful thinking—but was strangely silent when asked at what point his own prayer life turned sour. He had never learned to pray.

He dismissed Jesus as just a good man, then did a double take when I asked what he felt were the greatest marks of Jesus' manhood. My young friend was pained to admit he had never read the New Testament.

He was quick to inform me that the church's ideas about sex weren't important any more. I am still a little amused to remember the look on his face when he discovered how little he really knew about the Christian meaning of sex.

This is a strange irony, isn't it? One generation reacts against too much religion—and the next one doesn't even get a chance to make an intelligent decision as to whether it wants it.

In the Night

A little boy cries in the night. He is fevered and in pain and frightened by the dark.

And his father comes and takes his son in his arms.

The fever is still there and the pain is still there and the darkness is still there, but the little boy's sobbing gives way to a quiet restfulness now that his father has come.

Soon he is asleep again, and the healing powers within his body are once more at work in the wake of the healing of his troubled spirit.

Mankind is crying in the night. Men are morally sick and pained by hate and frightened by the world's darkness.

And the Father comes . . .

But men do not want to believe they need a Father. Men choose to believe they are orphans in a fatherless universe and their crying in the night only makes worse their sickness.

Still a Father waits to give the spirit that will cure

their sickness, the love that will take away the pains of hate, and the faith that will take away their fear of the dark. Then they could use the powers the Father has given them to overcome the world's darkness.

How long, O Father, will we shut you out with our stubbornness, our jealousies, our self-pity, our pride?

How long, O Father, will you stand beside us to help us, while we cry in the night and pretend you are not there?

As the Rioting Began

Blind *Passion* stalked down the streets of the city;
and *Reason* fled in dismay.

Prejudice slipped out of hiding to run wild in the simmering heat;
and *Justice* stood helpless a moment,
then hurried for the nearest exit.

Chaos took hold of the city, shaking it to the foundations;
and *Law* broke away from its clutches while
there was still time.

Cruelty walked up and down with a haughty sneer;
and *Mercy* hid in a dark alley till the mob passed
by and then fled.

Hate stormed through the town with a vengeance,
winning a victory over the masses;
but *Love* said, "These are still my people; I cannot
forsake them."

And so they looted and rioted and murdered; until
Love lay in the rubble, bleeding and broken.
And *Love* cried with a strange sense of knowing,
"I have been crucified before—and I will rise
again."

Summer Thoughts

Jesus left the city and went out into the wonder of
God's created world.

He met a few friends at the lakeside. They stepped
into the little fishing boat and went out to the deep
water.

They fished for awhile and talked of common
things. Peter mentioned how good it was to be here,
away from the crowds. It almost seemed they
were alone before God, taking in the wonder of what
he had created. They pulled in quite a string of fish
during the afternoon.

When they reached the shore, Jesus built a fire and cooked the meal. He taught them how to pray.

Then as the last coals burned out among the ashes and the meal was ended, they talked of eternal things; and Jesus gave to his friends power to live the life of love and forgiveness not only before their friends, but even before their enemies.

And they all went home refreshed and eager to take up the tasks that were set before them for the next day.

I left the city and went out into the wonder of God's created world.

I met a few friends at the lakeside. We stepped into the little fishing boat and went out to the deep water.

We fished for awhile, and got to telling smutty jokes. Some of them were real corkers! One of the guys thought a little bottled spirits would liven up the party, and another of the boys joined in to empty the bottle. We pulled in quite a string of bass, in spite of the dad-blamed mosquitoes and horseflies.

When we reached the shore, we built a fire and cooked the meal. Nobody bothered to say a prayer before we ate; it didn't seem to fit our mood.

Then as the last coals burned out among the ashes and the meal was ended, we got to talking about different people. One guy mentioned what a fool he made of his competitor. Another fellow started telling family secrets about one of his clients. We could hardly wait to tell the girls back home some of the scuttlebutt we picked up!

We were pretty well bushed by then so we loaded up the wagon and went home, dreading the thought of getting back into the old grind the next morning.

The Lamp of the American Dream

Timothy Bradford is one of the Mayflower descendants. He comes from sturdy stock.

During the bleak New England winter of 1621, William Bradford trudged through the snow and faced the biting wind to care for the sick and comfort the dying. When each Sunday dawned he stood in the little meeting house and praised the God who brought them to this wilderness, that their children might know the freedom to worship God in peace.

Yes, Timothy Bradford is a son of the Pilgrims who preys on mixed-up kids as a two-bit pusher.

And the lamp of the American dream flickers.

Tony Massasoit is a son of the first Americans. He comes from sturdy stock.

Chief Massasoit watched the strange boat pull into the bay and was amused at the stiff figures in black with the weird hats. During that first winter the Pilgrims would have starved had not the tall native chieftain taught them to make a stew from the clams

80

on the shore and shared with them his skills in the forest. As the new settlers took hold in the land and his people were sometimes honored and sometimes betrayed he said, "We have lived with the deer and the fox, we will learn to live with good and bad in the white man. We will not run and hide like rabbits."

Yes, Tony Massasoit is a son of the first Americans who finds life hard to handle and runs like a rabbit to his bottle.

And the lamp of the American dream flickers.

George Franklin is a son of the American Revolution. He comes from sturdy stock.

During the trying hours at Valley Forge, Tom Franklin bound up the wounds of the shivering soldiers and sang freedom songs he had learned from his black father on a Virginia plantation before a man named George Washington bought him his liberty. Tom stood tall and vowed he would never again be a slave to any man or any thing.

Yes, George Franklin is a son of the American Revolution who sells his soul for a needle of heroin and the dream world of forgetfulness.

And the lamp of the American dream flickers.

Juan Martinez is a son of the pioneers. He comes from sturdy stock.

Pablo Martinez was one of Coronado's men who stayed to colonize the New World. He joined forces with the Texans to declare his independence from Mexico, and he vowed before the altar of God that no man would ever call Pablo a dead-beat. In the years of drouth he tightened his belt and shared his meager beans and tortillas with the starving stranger, and he was honored as a man of integrity and goodwill.

Yes, Juan Martinez is a son of the pioneers who leeches on society as a petty thief.

And the lamp of the American dream flickers.

Bob Johnson is a son of the Republic. He comes from sturdy stock.

Thaddeus Johnson enlisted as a volunteer in the War between the States. Old Thad had two burning ideals—that the Union must be preserved and that every man's life is so sacred to God, you can't hate another man without damning yourself. He lost a leg in the war fighting for those ideals, yet he never questioned that it was worth it. But he not only fought for his ideals, Thad practiced them as long as he lived.

Yes, Bob Johnson is a son of the Republic and the loudest-mouthed bigot in Albuquerque.

And the lamp of the American dream flickers.

Let us remember that no race or group in America comes from stronger stock than another. All helped to make this nation great, and each of us at times has miserably failed his country.

On this Independence Day everyone of us—Chicano, Indian, Black, and White—had better get some fresh coal oil for the lamp of the American dream!

It's Only God!

Molly Jones relayed the purpose of her call to the freckle-faced boy who answered the doorbell. Unless she found a few more mothers to work in the classroom, they wouldn't be able to hold Vacation Church School. She knew how much the sessions meant to the children and hoped Mary Smith would help. Tommy went to get his mother, but she looked up from her movie magazine and whispered "Tell Molly I'm not feeling well—I'll call her later."

But what she really said was: *Never mind—it's only God. He can wait.*

Jeanie Smith came into the den where her dad was reading the sports page and brought her church school workbook. In one section of the lesson, the father is supposed to help his child read the scripture selection and answer some questions. Joe Smith turned aside from the paper long enough to say, "Jeanie, can't you see I'm busy?"

But what he really said was: *Never mind—it's only God. He can wait!*

The pastor made a luncheon appointment with Mack Tucker. He laid before the businessman some crying needs of a deprived neighborhood in the shadow of their church. Mack leaned back in his chair and shook his head, "Preacher, are you still on that do-gooder kick? I thought you had something important to talk about."

But what he really said was: *Never mind—it's only God. He can wait!*

Ted Johnson had just settled down in front of the TV set when his phone rang. The wife of an old friend asked if he could come over. Her husband was talking of suicide and Ted was the only man he would listen to. Looking off into space the man answered, "I'm sorry, but we're doing inventory tonight. I have to rush back to the store." He put down the phone and returned to his easy chair for the rest of the evening.

But what he really said was: *Never mind—it's only God. He can wait!*

When Jesus Took a Vacation
I. A Trip to the Mountains

It was summer. The days were long and the heat of the desert wastes blew in on Caesarea Philippi. Jesus turned aside from the crowds and went away to the mountains with a few close friends.

The cypress trees swayed in the cool breeze on a little ridge. A clear stream flowed at their feet, splashing against the boulders in its path. And the rugged granite cliffs rose high above them just beyond the stream.

Peter marveled at the beauty of the everlasting hills as he said, "Surely God is in this place."

But Jesus said, "If you really want to see God working, come with me."

Peter wondered what spot in the mountains Jesus had seen that maybe he missed—except to his dismay they were going down from the mountains, back to the heat, the dust, and the sweaty crowds at Caesarea. As they approached the town, a man was waiting with an afflicted son. Jesus touched the boy and made him well again.

And Peter mused to himself, "It's hard to get used to the idea that we're closest to God when we meet him in the needs of our brother."

Have you met him there?

When Jesus Took a Vacation
II. A Fishing Trip

It was late September. The autumn leaves had just begun to turn into a magic blaze of color against the backdrop of the hills. Jesus walked away from the little Nazareth carpenter shop and went fishing.

A sea gull soared over the waters of the lake as ever so often a whitecap broke on a wave. Peter and John called from their boats offshore to say they had fished for hours and nothing was biting. Jesus asked them to try once more fishing from the other side of the boat, and they pulled in so many fish they almost sank.

Peter was thunderstruck as he said, "Lord, with you along, we can make a first-class operation out of this fishing business."

But Jesus said, "No, Peter, from here, we go to the bigger thrill of fishing for men!"

Peter wondered what he meant by that until he saw the Master take fear out of the eyes of a lonely, desperate man.

Peter mused to himself, "It never struck me that a fisherman could get a bigger thrill helping a man find God than pulling a bass into his boat."

You can do both, you know! Have you?

When Jesus Took a Vacation
III. At a Winter Resort

It was December. The days were cold in the little mountain village as the winter wind blew in off the lake. Jesus closed the door of the house in which he was staying as he carried out his tasks of healing and teaching, and he and his friends took a few days vacation to the town of Jericho at the edge of the desert.

The palm trees lined in splendor the streets of the winter resort. The warmth of the sun touched the sights of the town with beauty for these strangers from the north. And the fame of Jesus had spread even to this little town so that people came to hear his matchless words of truth.

Peter said, "This is wonderful! The crowds hear you every place we go! You're not a stranger anywhere!"

But Jesus said, "Peter, I have something more important to do than draw a crowd."

Peter was wondering what he meant by that when he saw the Master stop and single out a grubby little cheat named Zacchaeus and go home with him for dinner.

Peter mused to himself, "I never thought before that even the people we don't like are worth saving."

Did it ever occur to you?

When Jesus Took a Vacation
IV. In the Nation's Capital

It was spring. The lilies of the field cast a spell of beauty over the countryside, and the turtledoves were singing from the forest trees. Jesus and the Twelve went up from Galilee one day to Jerusalem.

The ancient city of the kings of Israel was a place of wonder to these small-town men. They were caught up in the spell of the rush and busyness of the market-place. They stared in awe at the massive buildings in the heart of the city.

Peter said, "What buildings—what a big place!"

But Jesus was strangely unimpressed with the bigness of it all as he called their attention to a widow giving everything she had as a gesture of love and gratitude before God, for the sake of others.

Peter mused to himself, "Jesus must grow weary of trying to make us see that people are bigger than buildings in the sight of God."

Do you find it hard to remember that people are more important than things?

What Price Success?

Chuck Weaver has established himself as one of the most competent authorities in the field of human relations and methods of communication. He is sought by the biggest corporations in the nation to hold seminars for executives. His popularity on the lecture circuit is a source of genuine pride to him. Such success did not come without diligent study and years of hard, grinding preparation.

But there is gnawing on Chuck a haunting fear that he may be losing his wife. With all his expertise in telling other people about human relations, he hasn't really been able to talk to Mary for the last couple of years.

My friend, there is no other kind of success that will make up for failure in the home!

Jane Smith makes her associates feel that some people are born with a natural ability to get things done. If a leader is needed to organize the Mother's March—call Jane. If the P.T.A. needs a president who will carry the ball for public education right up the Governor's office—call Jane. Whatever the community needs in the way of volunteer service by a dedicated, efficient woman—call Jane. No person in the city has won the admiration of people more than she.

But Jane was really shaken when she woke up one day to the fact that her son had been on hard drugs for a year, and she hadn't even suspected it.

My friend, there is no other kind of success that will make up for failure in the home!

Jimmy Davis was the best athlete Sandia High ever had. He worked at making a name for himself. He was picked for the quarterback slot as a sophomore and guided the team brilliantly to football championships his last two years. Yet, he still worked in enough time for basketball practice to become high-point man as a senior. He was voted player of the year and won the plaudits of sports writers across the state.

But during those years Jimmy so humiliated his younger brother for acting like a sissy that the boy will carry emotional scars the rest of his life.

My friend, there is no other kind of success that will make up for failure in the home!

What Do You Look For?

What do you look for in a person whom you meet on the street? I wonder if the things you find in a man are the things you were looking for! Could that be a part of the problems that torment us—our low expectations of each other? Go back with me across the centuries . . .

He was a big man—the outdoor type, and the strong smell of the handling of fish nets clung to him. He was crude and vulgar and thoughtless in his speech.

So the people of Capernaum looked on Simon of Galilee.

But Jesus saw behind the rough exterior the kind of strength and integrity God could use in a wishy-washy world. And Simon Peter became what Jesus believed he could become.

The woman lingered on the street corner and cast an inviting glance to the stranger from Nazareth.

All the respectable folk scorned the harlot as they lifted the skirts of their robes and stepped out into the street to make sure that even her shadow did not fall on them.

So the people of the city looked on Mary of Magdala.

But Jesus saw behind the painted face with the forced smile a woman who needed someone to love her for the sake of her own worth and not for her body. And Mary the Magdalene became more pure in soul than the self-righteous ones of the city, because of the faith the Master had in her.

The little man behind the desk was as weak in character as he was in body. He had sold out his own people to collect taxes for the Roman Army of occupation. There was no contempt great enough to shower on such scum as the publicans.

So the people of the city looked on Matthew.

But Jesus saw behind the smug mask of the prosperous tax-collector the heart of a lonely man who despaired at having sold his soul and his country so cheaply. Jesus believed this man was still a child of God who had so much to give if only someone would be God's friend to him. And the beauty of Matthew's Gospel is eloquent tribute that the faith the Master placed in him was justified.

Friend . . . could it be that many will walk through life lonely and lost and tortured, for no other reason than that you and I refused to see them through the eyes of Christ?

That Generation Gap!

As I look back across the centuries to the men of the Bible, there was no one who loved his country more than Jeremiah, yet no man felt more deeply the heartbreak of his fellow men who had missed the purpose of his country's birth.

I, too, love my country—yet I, too, cry for the people of America. I am concerned that my generation cannot talk to our children. I am amazed that we cannot understand why they are confused and bewildered, and sometimes lost and sometimes bitter, with the feeling they must protest against the times into which they were born.

I am amazed—but I suppose I shouldn't be. Can we ever see ourselves as the future will judge us?

Let me tell you what is bothering me. One of your sons came to my office last week. Will you dare to hear what your son wanted to know?

Your son asked why we talk about the importance of law and order, yet pay no attention to traffic laws unless we see a policeman in the rear-view mirror.

Your son asked why we say "In God we trust," yet our churches stand half-empty on Sunday morning.

Your son asked why we complain about graft and corruption in high places, yet are willing to exaggerate losses on insurance claims for a few dishonest dollars.

Your son asked why we spend more for tobacco and alcohol than for teachers' salaries, then piously claim we believe in the importance of a good education for the youth of today.

Your son asked why we talk about the dignity of work, yet make a man feel inferior if he isn't in one of the "prestige occupations."

Your son asked why old men start wars and force young men to die for a cause they don't believe in.

Your son asked why we talk about the infinite worth of every person in the sight of God, yet we don't really mean that if a man's face is a different color from our own.

Your son asked why we get so upset about changing sex patterns, yet can't find time to show a kind of love and caring in the home that would help them know how to handle sex.

Your son asked why we become so righteous in condemning marijuana, then retreat into the twilight world of an alcoholic "high."

Your son asked why we say "there are some things money can't buy," then turn and sell our souls for social and material success.

I don't like to answer these questions—but until you and I are willing to wrestle with them, we can't begin to close that generation gap.

The Dilemma

A major American oil company felt the need for an in-depth study of its operations in one of the countries of South America. When the study was completed, the report urged that more native personnel be involved in the decision-making and managerial positions if the company were to operate at its maximum efficiency. The officials of the oil company agreed with the findings and prepared to put them into effect.

But just as they were ready to announce the new policy, a group of radical leftists in the capital of the nation carried out a violent demonstration against the presence of the American operators of the oil company in their country.

Now the dilemma—if the company went ahead with its plans, many people would think they were responding to the pressures of the militant leftists. But if a policy is right, should it not be implemented? The company decided to go ahead with the needed change, even though some would not understand their real motives.

A great Southern university felt the need for an in-depth study of its curriculum and decision-making processes. When the study was completed, one of the recommendations called for more involvement of the students and faculty in setting goals and priorities for a good education. The President and Board of Trustees agreed with the findings and prepared to put them into effect.

But just as they were ready to announce the new practices, a group of radical leftists in the university carried out a violent demonstration demanding more student rights.

Now the dilemma—if the university went ahead with its plan, many people would think they were responding to the pressures of the militant leftists. But if a policy is right, should it not be implemented? The university decided to go ahead with the needed reforms, even though some would not understand their real motives.

The United Methodist Church felt the need for an in-depth study of ways it could best minister to the needs of its almost half a million Black members in this difficult period in the life of America. When the study was completed, one recommendation was that certain mission funds be given the church's Black leadership to be used in helping their fellow Black Americans grow toward a new sense of dignity and Christian responsibility. The Mission Board of the Church agreed with the findings and prepared to put them into effect.

But just as they were ready to announce the new program, a group of radical leftists delivered to the white churches and synagogues of America a violent Black Manifesto demanding millions of dollars in reparations for previous wrongs done to the Black man.

Now the dilemma—if the Board of Missions went ahead with its plans, many people would think they were responding to the pressures of the militant leftists. But if a policy is right, should it not be implemented? The Board decided to go ahead with the needed program, even though some would not understand their real motives.

Men of goodwill in every field of American life—
business, education, religion—need our understanding and our prayers. Do they have yours?

Celebrating Our Own Destruction

Hurricane Camille raged her relentless way across
the Gulf of Mexico in a direct path toward the coast of
Mississippi. The warnings to evacuate were radioed
to all the inhabitants of the coastal cities of the Mag-
nolia State, and in a steady stream of traffic the evac-
uees moved northward from the coast.

But in the Richelieu Apartments overlooking the
Gulf, twenty-three tenants were making preparations
for a hurricane party to ride out the storm. After all,
the sturdy brick structure was hurricane proof. And
so, as the storm slashed the shores with winds at 190
miles per hour, twenty-three people were using the
hurricane as a means of having a party. Then suddenly, it was all over, and the party guests had become only statistics in the storm's grisly death toll.

How foolish, you say? Using your destroyer as the
theme for a party?

Yes, but I know many who do the same thing day
by day. One man's destroyer is unbridled sex. Another man's destroyer is a lust for power. Some make

96

a party of hating. Some make a party out of prejudice. A woman plays games with gossip. A youth plays games with his cheating. Maybe you can add to the list of destroyers in the lives of people.

But I have a better idea—make your list personal! Is there something you take lightly that is destroying your image as a child of God? Are you really any wiser than the tenants of the Richelieu Apartments who threw a hurricane party and perished in their hurricane-proof home?

Have You Been There?

In the little town of Bethlehem, people on the street would pass a mother with her child and smile and say, "What a beautiful baby."

But one night, when a poor woman needed a place to shelter her child from the cold, there was no room for her baby in their homes.

In the village of Nazareth, a young man stood to speak, and everybody smiled and said, "Isn't it wonderful that one of our hometown boys has become a preacher?"

But there came a day when the young Jesus made them see they only talked about God and didn't really believe in him enough to change their ways of living. And his townspeople became so furious they tried to throw him off a cliff.

In the city of Jerusalem a crowd of bystanders sang psalms of praise, clapped their hands and smiled to welcome the Stranger from Galilee. And they said, "Isn't it wonderful to see and hear so great a man."

But during the next four days, Jesus showed they were all so interested in themselves, they couldn't care less how they treated the rest of God's children. And they were so guilt-ridden they called him a criminal and nailed him to a tree, hoping to cover up the selfishness in their hearts he had so painfully exposed to view.

Dear Friend, have you ever stood with the passers-by in Bethlehem—or Nazareth—or Jerusalem?

Kingdomtide

□□□

The season of proclamation that the kingdoms of this world have become the kingdom of our Lord and of his Christ.

It Was Only . . .

It was only a shabby stable
    Beyond an ancient inn,
But it speaks the Beauty in common things
    Since Love was born therein.

It was only a brawny fisherman
    Beside Lake Galilee,
But the joy he found as a friend of God
    Is open to you and me.

It was only a lily in the field
    That bloomed along the way,
But it grew as a sign that God is good,
    And his gifts are ours today.

It was only a coarse, wood cross
    That stood upon a hill,
But in earth's dark hour it flamed with a Light
    That pierces the darkness still.

It was only an empty tomb
    Outside Jerusalem,
But it tells of a God who will not die,
    However we bury him.

The Carpenter

The Carpenter stood to teach and his listeners marveled, "No one ever spoke like this before."

The Carpenter walked along the lakeshore and stopped at the water's edge to preach, "and the great throng heard him gladly."

The Carpenter knelt beside a guilty sinner and wrote in the sand, "Let him who is without sin among you be the first to throw a stone," and the woman's accusers knew he had ripped away the mask of their self-righteousness, as they dropped their stones.

The Carpenter sat at the wailing wall and prophesied the fall of the city of David because of the nation's fickle ways before God, and the people trembled as his judgments came home to each of them.

But mark this well—no one would have listened to the Carpenter at all if, in Nazareth, he had built shoddy houses.

What does your workmanship say about your witness?

A Parent's Prayer as College Begins

Tomorrow, Father, our firstborn will be leaving home. We have saved and planned for this time when she goes away to college, but suddenly we discover that you never completely get ready for the great moments in life. Last May when she finished high school she seemed so grown, and now that she prepares to go away from us, she seems so young again.

But that's always been your problem with doting fathers, hasn't it? This is that joyous moment she was born for. You tried to make our purpose clear to us: we were to surround her with love, give her firm but thoughtful discipline, fill her days with work and laughter, live out a faith in her presence, so that one day she could make it on her own when we were not there to stand beside her. And now that day has come.

Thank you, Father, for these years together. Thank you for all the laughter and tears, all the joy and the wonder of them.

And now be with her and with us and help us all to keep on growing. For we have so great a Love that holds us together, nothing can ever really separate us in the things that matter.

Thank you for this greatest gift.

Eyes to See

Jesus saw a field of lilies and gave thanks to God as the Creator of such loveliness.

—We see a field of lilies and try to figure how we can improve on it by laying out a concrete playground.

Jesus found a quiet spot of beauty on the lakeside where he and the disciples could go for moments of renewal.
—We find a quiet spot of beauty on the lakeside and turn it into a honky-tonk with booming noises, in order to make a fast buck.

Jesus saw the wonder of God's world as a priceless gift to be used reverently and passed on to our children as clean and fruitful as we received it.
—We see the world as our plaything to erode and pollute and make ugly, and we call subversive anyone who dares to question our right to do so.

Jesus talked about a man who was a fool because he had great possessions, but was not rich toward God.
—We spend our time trying to secure more possessions, and think a man is a fool to waste his time worrying about values that can't be converted into hard cash.

Jesus looked at the skyline of a big city and was unimpressed; but he couldn't forget the haunting picture of a child in rags sharing a cup of cold water with a cripple at the temple gate.
—We are impressed with the mass of concrete and steel in the towers that rise above the city, and we

pass by the poor in the streets as though they didn't even exist.

O God, give us eyes to see, before it is too late.

A Time to Play and a Time to Refrain from Playing

It came every year to Jerusalem—the Feast of the Passover. For eight days the city was astir with all the excitement. Children looked forward to it with wonder-filled thoughts of all the fun there would be at the celebration. This did not mean that everyone came only to play. There were many who remembered the purpose of the Passover celebration. And of course, there is nothing wrong with play in itself— unless people let the playing cause them to forget their moral obligations.

One Passover in Jerusalem it happened that way. Normally good men, caught up in the mood of the crowd, became a party to deeds that made them forget their moral obligations.

One man sold out a friend for thirty pieces of silver.

One man joined in with a crowd of people who were cruelly taunting a "mad carpenter" from a country town.

One man, just for the sport of it, took the platform
as a false witness against a prisoner whom he
really didn't know.

One man blew a month's rent money gambling for
the seamless robe of the crucified Jesus.

Thinking he was lost in the celebrating crowd, each
man let himself forget he was a son of God.

It comes every year to Albuquerque—the State
Fair. For ten days the city is astir with all the excitement. Children look forward to it with wonder-filled
thoughts of all the fun there will be at the celebration.
This does not mean that everyone comes only to play.
There are many who remember the purpose of a
State Fair. And, of course, there is nothing wrong
with play in itself—unless people let the playing
cause them to forget their moral obligations.

One State Fair week in Albuquerque it happened
that way. Normally good men, caught up in the mood
of the crowd, became a party to deeds that made them
forget their moral obligations.

One man spent more money betting on the horses
than he gave in a whole year for causes of Christian compassion.

One man who left his wife at home made out with
a young girl in the shadow of a booth on the mid-
way.

One man spent what he could not afford, and
caused his hard-pressed creditors to sweat out
for months whether they would ever be repaid.

One man got drunk and made everyone miserable
with his abusiveness.

Thinking he was lost in the celebrating crowd, each man let himself forget he was a son of God.

Have you learned to enjoy the festivals of life, and still be true to your moral obligations?

"Do This in Remembrance of Me"

I take these symbols in my hand: Bread and wine—
  food to eat and drink—
  such common things!
Yet, without food to eat and drink,
  I should surely die.

And He said, "This is my body!"—
  not just flesh and blood—
A body is more than this!

Christ is also: Words and deeds—
  judging, yet forgiving—
  knowing, yet loving—
  dying, yet living!
Without these—of which the bread and wine are
    symbols—
  I shall surely die!

How Jesus Taught

They were all sitting around, talking men's talk—
and Jesus put a child in their midst.

The men were growing careless in their conduct and
their conversation—
and Jesus put a child in their midst.

The Twelve began to feel they had learned all they
needed to know to be good diciples—
and Jesus put a child in their midst.

Some of them were flirting with the idea of "limited
violence" to bring in the kingdom of God—
and Jesus put a child in their midst.

His followers were getting anxious to reach the business community and the "right people"—
and Jesus put a child in their midst.

The twelve men took a long look
   at their arrogance
     and their careless deeds
      and their need to learn
       and the consequences of their actions
        and the worth of a human soul—
because Jesus put a child in their midst.

What Does a Young Man Do?

What does a Christian do when war comes? There are no easy answers. Jesus once said to the Twelve, "Let him who has no sword sell his mantle and buy one"; yet his last words to Peter were, "Put your sword back into its place; for all who take the sword will perish by the sword." Jesus praised the devout faith of a Roman soldier, yet he was crucified by another soldier carrying out orders. How does a man honor both God and his country?

His country was at war. Tom sat down with his New Testament and wrestled with the decision as to what he should do. He didn't believe in killing. What does a Christian do? He had learned as a young boy to pray—even for his enemies. But he had followed the progress of his country's entry into the war and he believed his nation's leaders had no other choice. He looked on the actions of the enemy as a crime against humanity and he saw innocent millions suffering from those actions. He turned to his Bible again and read the words of Jesus, "Render to Caesar the things that are Caesar's, and to God the things that are God's." He prayed for guidance and felt his duty to both his country and his God called him to serve in the armed forces.

Tom gave his life for his convictions when a piece of shrapnel hit him on the road leading into Dachau.

His country was at war. Jim sat down with his New Testament and wrestled with the decision as to what he should do. He didn't believe in killing. What should a Christian do? He had learned as a young boy to pray—even for his enemies. He was not a coward, but the words of the commandment "Thou shalt not kill" kept thundering in his conscience. He turned to the words of Jesus, "All who take the sword will perish by the sword." But he also despised the actions of the enemy his country was fighting. He prayed for guidance and enlisted in the army, asking for assignment as a noncombatant for reasons of Christian conscience. He was assigned to the medical corps.

Jim gave his life for his convictions as he lifted a wounded soldier into his arms and a sniper's bullet hit him in the temple.

His country was at war. John sat down with his New Testament and wrestled with the decision as to what he should do. He didn't believe in killing. What should a Christian do? He had learned as a young boy to pray—even for his enemies. He was no coward. He had never taken part in violence of any kind. He tried to take Jesus completely at his word. It had not been easy, but he had tried literally to do what his Master said: "If anyone strikes you on the right cheek, turn to him the other also." He prayed for guidance, and felt that he must refuse any part in his country's war effort. He entered a government prison and began serving his sentence. After several months he was invited to share in a medical research experiment to try to find a cure for polio. The choice was his, but he was glad to be a part of the experiment. He was given the inoculation and then infected with the polio germ. Something about the timing of the experiment was off.

John gave his life for his convictions in a British prison hospital.

His country was at war. Peter sat down with his New Testament and wrestled with the decision as to what he should do. He didn't believe in killing. What does a Christian do? He had learned as a boy to pray—even for his enemies. He was no coward. He had served in his country's navy several years before, and been decorated for bravery. Why should his conscience bother him now? He had studied the issues, and he didn't believe his country had any business in this particular war. This time he believed his country was wrong. He turned to his Bible again and read the words of the early Christians, "We must obey God rather than man." He refused to bear arms in a cause in which he could not believe, and he was sent to prison.

Peter gave his life not long after that at the hands of the executioner in a Nazi concentration camp.

What does a young Christian do when war comes? So long as we put a Bible in his hands and ask him to pray for guidance, there are young men who will choose at one time or another these four different ways of witnessing to their Christian faith. Only God can say whether each man has chosen the right way. But as a Christian I must respect the right of each man to be honored for choosing which of the four decisions will be his.

Second Thoughts

As he drove to work this morning, Tom Blocker was still boiling over the sermon his pastor had preached on Sunday. He didn't like for a minute the insinuation that every Christian should consider tithing his income. "Talk about sacrifice!" he muttered.

Just then Tom saw a billboard with the picture of a cross towering over a broken world.

Mary Smith was drinking a leisurely cup of coffee after getting the children off to school, when the phone rang. It was Martha Thompson recruiting canvassers for the Stewardship Crusade. She was quick-witted enough to find an excuse to beg off this time, and as she hung up the receiver she thought, "I don't have time for all I want to do, let alone that kind of busywork."

Just then Mary glanced down at the beautiful cross she was wearing around her neck.

Tim Vickers opened a letter from the church telling about the services offered his children, as well as older people with real needs. Then there was the clincher, calling the members to increase their giving. He let out a mild oath as he concluded, "They're always asking for more money!"

Just then he looked out the window of his office building to see a huge cross on a church steeple.

And suddenly three people had some second thoughts about their scale of values when they saw things in the light of a cross!

112

So They Dreamed

"I never will forget the night he was born, there in that horrid innyard with the stable smells and the cold night air blowing in through the chinks of the walls. But look at my son now, growing up in these Judean hills, strong and fine and handsome. Someday he will make his mark on the world." So dreamed Mary the mother of Jesus.

"I never will forget the night he was born, there in the villa with the bewildered servants running in and out of the courtyard, and that bungling midwife . . . he's lucky to be alive. But look at my son now, growing up amid the hills of Rome, strong and fine and handsome. Someday he will make his mark on the world." So dreamed the mother of Pontius Pilate.

"I never will forget the night he was born, there in the little cottage by the wayside where the gentle night breezes tempered the summer heat and the song of a lark was the lullaby for my frail son. But look at him now, growing up on the plains of Kerioth, strong and fine and handsome. Someday he will make his mark on the world." So dreamed the mother of Judas Iscariot.

O youth, who look on the future as yours to mold,
O youth, with your innocent idealism,
O strong and fine and handsome youth of today,
Do not forget these three men—and remember,
Decision determines destiny!

What Happened to Linda?

A young girl was found dead in the basement of a hippie flophouse in Greenwich Village. Why did she choose to live as a hippie? What fascination drew her to this strange dream world? What happened to Linda? I wonder . . . could it be . . . ?

Linda was born into a home where nothing was spared to fulfill the desires of her heart. The house in the suburbs rang with the laughter of her friends as they danced to rock and splashed in the big blue swimming pool on the beautifully landscaped grounds.
What more could a young girl ask for?

Linda shared the special privileges of a private school. There were the weekend parties, good-natured competition in athletics, and festive dances at the country club. Life was one thrilling social event after another.
What more could a young girl ask for?

Linda went with the family on the summer vacations. There were cruises to the Antilles, trips to the Florida coast, and those wonderful weeks in Bermuda with swimming, beach parties, painting, and sight-seeing around the island.
What more could a young girl ask for?

Linda was not spared the fruits of her father's good fortune. There were shopping expeditions, special

114

attention at a salon where the hairdresser kept her in style, the smart shops in New York whose buyers saw that she was dressed in the latest fashions.

What more could a young girl ask for?

But one day, Linda stepped back and looked at her world. It suddenly seemed so shallow that she asked herself, "Is this *all* there is to living? Is there contentment money can't buy? Is there a life that's caring for people nobody else cares for? Is there Something worth giving yourself to that's bigger than you are?

Linda started looking! I don't know why, but she thought she saw in the hippies people who were looking for the same answers.

Somehow, it never occurred to Linda that the church might be able to help her find those answers.

O God, why? Why didn't she think we might have some answers?

Please, God, help us to find out why.

Asking the Right Questions

Once long ago . . .

Herod the king walked out on the balcony of the palace and looked at the stars. The nights in Israel were beautiful as the rolling hills nestled against the horizon. But it was hard for a king to enjoy his kingdom when he was only a puppet of the Romans. He remembered in the scriptures of Israel that someday a Messiah would appear. "O God," he cried into the night, "When will you come to drive out this hated army of Rome, and let me be king of the Jews in my own right?"

Aaron the priest passed the row of beggars at the temple gate and flung a coin at each one as he went by. Many of these wretches were soldiers wounded in recent skirmishes with the Roman invaders. But this was not all the occupation had done to them. He scowled at the influx of strangers the conquerors allowed to walk their streets—arrogant Greeks, the mixed-breed Samaritans, black-faced Cyrenians. What irony that he should be walking through the temple gate called "beautiful" when such people passed by the gate to defile its beauty. He remembered in the scriptures of Israel that someday a Messiah would appear, and he prayed, "O God, when will you come and drive from our land these foreigners whom you hate as we do? How long, O Lord, before you vindicate your chosen ones and destroy our enemies?"

The innkeeper sat in his office and pored over the accounts. Taxes were taking an ever-increasing bite of his profits. It was hard to get good help. The old building was sadly in need of repairs, but with this uncertain economy he wouldn't dare borrow money to expand. The country needed something. He remembered in the scriptures of Israel that someday a

Messiah would appear, and he muttered, 'O God, when are you going to come and bring us security? Then we would know that you love us."

And the Christ came—but each man had his own image of what a messiah should be—and each man looked into the heart of God and never knew He was there.

But it happened that . . .

A woman looked out her kitchen window and watched the children at play. She thought of the good in the heart of a child if only it could be directed to ways of peace as he grows older. Then she thought of the wars and the violence in her homeland. She remembered in the scriptures of Israel that someday a Messiah would appear. And she prayed, "O God, when will you come and give us at least the vision of a kingdom where men do not turn to the agony of war to cover their failure to be statesmen?"

A cripple at the temple gate looked at the people passing by. There was no place for the handicapped in the economy of Judea, except to beg. It was bad enough to be an invalid, but the daily scorn of those who considered their suffering a punishment of God was an indignity which left him desolate. Only his fellow beggars knew the depths of his loneliness. Then he remembered in the scriptures of Israel that someday a Messiah would appear. And he cried, "O God, I could bear the crippling and the agony of pain, if only I know someone cared. Will you ever come, to care for outcasts like me?"

A harlot on a city street tightened the cloak around

her shoulders as the wind blew between the buildings. But colder this day than the winter winds were the stares of contempt from the righteous ones of the city who knew her profession. Why does a woman sell her body? she often asked that question. It was not the money alone. She could have married the rich old man her father bartered for and had security. But something in the soul of the harlot cried out for love. At least there were those who loved her for her body. But shouldn't there be a Love you don't have to sell your body to find? She remembered in the scriptures of Israel that someday a Messiah would appear. And she spoke under her breath, "O God, could you come and show us what Love is—a Love that is more than passion and kinder than charity?"

And the Christ came—and out of their desperate longing, each of the three looked into the heart of God and found what each was seeking.

Still he comes and stands among us. Are you asking the right questions to find him?

With Apologies to Women's Lib

Mr. Kelly was not a handsome man. He was short and a little paunchy. His dark hair was beginning to gray around the edges and showed signs of thinning in the middle. He had bushy black eyebrows that could have been frightening had he been the kind to scowl at you, and his voice was husky like the graveled tones of the gangster-types in the old Saturday afternoon movies. Yet, for all this forbidding exterior, there was a time in my life when I thought this man was one of the world's heroes.

Mr. Kelly was my third-grade Sunday school teacher. I don't remember what we studied when I was a wiggly, well-washed child in my not too comfortable Sunday best. Much of what we learn is picked up so unconsciously that we would all be hard-put to recall the source. I do remember that Mr. Kelly took us fishing one Saturday afternoon in a little farm pond. But there were other teachers who took us on class outings, so there had to be something more in the magic halo this man wore.

I suppose in looking back, a part of his influence was the fact a grown man believed in God enough to come and talk about him to a bunch of squirming third-grade kids. All my teachers at school were women. I hoped to be a man someday—and it was great to see that real men believe in God too!

Are there any heroes in the church today like Mr. Kelly—men who will come around to let boys in grade school know that believing in God is not just kid stuff? Are there any volunteers around to help my son know that real men still believe in God!

Point of View

A small cluster of men, women, and children stood shivering on the shore as the fog hovered over the British coast at Plymouth. These Pilgrims of faith had hoped for freedom to worship according to their conscience and had failed to find that hope fulfilled in their own country first, and later in Holland. They were prepared now to begin a voyage that promised a nightmarish Atlantic crossing and an unwelcome winter in a strange, unsettled land.

But in that lonely, uncertain hour, one of their number spoke for the entire company, "God has yet more light to break forth from his word."

They looked on the troubles at hand, and saw not difficulties, but opportunities.

A small boy sat beside a roaring fire in a rough, frame cabin, reading from a borrowed book. His father was a drifter, one of the restless pioneers who was always looking for a better place to put down stakes, and never finding it. There were only two books in the home—Shakespeare's works and the Bible but the boy read them again and again so that their lessons were imprinted on his conscience. He had little schooling, and his family heritage held no promise of a better life than his father knew.

But young Abraham Lincoln wrote in the flyleaf of the first book he ever owned, "I will study and prepare myself and someday my chance will come."

He looked on the hopelessness at hand and saw not despair, but an opportunity.

The bombs rained down on London. Everywhere there was death and destruction. Some of the most treasured achievements of the centuries lay in ruins. There was doubt that England would survive this war.

But one day Winston Churchill stood in the rubble of the battered city and said, "Let us . . . so bear ourselves that, if the British Empire and its Commonwealth last for a thousand years, men will still say: this was their finest hour."

He looked on the destruction at hand and saw not defeat but an opportunity.

This is one of God's greatest gifts to the human spirit. Cherish it.

Brothers Under the Skin

Tim Morgan didn't believe the Black man had been given a fair shake. He wrote to his congressman, and talked himself blue in the face, and everybody said, "We're working at it. Be patient, Black boy."

So Tim sweated out the long, hot summer. He

lived with the stink of the rats and the roaches. He took the "smart" of loudmouthed white trash until he had a belly full.

He decided to take things into his own hands as he joined a gang one night that threw a Molotov cocktail into one store window and another and another. Before morning came he had burned and looted until his pent-up anger was satisfied, and he gloated over the spoils of the evening.

Nick Washington didn't believe the Black man had gotten a fair shake. He wrote to his congressman and talked himself blue in the face, and everybody said, "Be patient, Black boy. We're working at it, but it takes time."

So Nick sweated out the long, hot summer. He lived with the stink of the rats and the roaches. He took the "smart" of loudmouthed white trash until he had a belly full.

Nick thought of taking to the streets, but the demonstrations had lost their punch, and his own people suffered most in the riots. Nick thought, "There's got to be a better way!" He called together some men of goodwill—both white and black, as he said, "We resent not getting the freedom everybody talks about, but we want it the right way. Will you help us find the answers!"

And together they forged a new day of hope for the Black men of the city to come into their own.

John Smith believed in law and order. He had a belly full of people disobeying the law because they couldn't get what they wanted. He was especially angry with the violence in his own city streets that he was sure had roots in the Black ghetto.

He wrote to his congressman and talked himself blue in the face, and he wasn't satisfied with the answers he was getting.

So John decided to take the law into his own hands. He bought a pistol and kept it in easy reach. One night when the city was restless and it looked as though there might be a demonstration, he slipped down the street to where the action was. The police were trying hard to "keep their cool," when John saw one insolent fellow making an obscene gesture. He took a bead on him, let fire, and slipped off unnoticed. The riot was under way, and John was hoping the police would have an excuse now to mop up the whole gang of troublemakers.

Ralph Jordan believed in law and order. He had a belly full of people disobeying the law because they couldn't get what they wanted. He was especially angry with the violence in his own city streets that he was sure had roots in the Black ghetto.

He wrote to his congressman and talked himself blue in the face, and he wasn't satisfied with the answers he was getting.

So Ralph sat down one day with a police officer, a member of the city council, and a man who knew how people felt in the ghetto. He found the problem wasn't quite so simple as one might think. Some of it had to do with the way troublemakers were raised in the home, without love or discipline. He was reminded of men who say, "Support your local police," but aren't willing to tax themselves to secure more police, with better training, and to set up a crime laboratory. He also discovered some people had real grievances. When Ralph saw the whole story, he quit bellyaching about "law and order" and began helping to solve some problems—without taking the law into his own hands.

Two sets of men were brothers under the skin . . . but the men who were *really* brothers didn't have the same color of skin!

And So a Man Says

In every age some men have lived as though God did not matter, whether through despair or a blind trust in their own powers. Our age is hardly different from any other.

So a man says, "I know it's a rough way to live, but it doesn't bother them the way it would us. And besides, think how much better off they are now than they were before they came here. I just think when God made the different races he planned for some to lead and others to follow."

124

And in the presence of the Egyptian landowner, *God raised up a man named Moses.*

So a man says, "They don't make statesmen any more. I remember when we had great leaders at the head of the government. The other countries didn't look down their noses at us in those days. I sometimes wonder if God even cares what happens to his chosen nation."

And in the presence of the disillusioned Israelite, *God raised up a king named Hezekiah.*

So a man says, "It's a good life we have, but it didn't come easy. I remember when things were rough. We had to pull ourselves up by our own boot-straps. So it took hard work—if I could do it, any-body can. Don't needle me about my responsibility to God. If I'd waited for him to supply my needs, I'd still be a pauper. God can be your hobby—I want something a little more tangible."

And in the presence of the prosperous Jew in Baby-lon, *God raised up an exile named Isaiah.*

So a man says, "Weapons—that's the way it has to be done. Those guys don't know any other lan-guage. The old boys in religion can talk all they want to about loving your neighbor, but we've never run up against this kind of neighbor before. A well-measured dose of hate has its place in this kind of world. If we have to be like them to win, then what are we waiting for? After we whip them, then we

can start all over again learning to love our neighbors."

And in the presence of the Zealots in Jerusalem,
God raised up a carpenter named Jesus.

For Times Like These

When I was in grade school our class was given
the assignment of memorizing Kipling's "If." There
was a phrase in the poem which had little meaning
for me then:

If you can bear to hear the truth you've spoken
Twisted by knaves to make a trap for fools,
Or watch the things you gave your life to, broken,
And stoop and build 'em up with worn-out tools . . .

But with the passing years those words take on an
ever deeper meaning. So much of life is a matter of
broken dreams:

A research scientist at a major American university
had almost completed a project of great concern.
His findings were recorded on computer tapes. Then
in a senseless night of violence by radical activists on
the campus, his lifework was destroyed. *And a lonely
man sat in the shambles of his broken dreams.*

A man of integrity reviewed his blueprint for reforms that were long overdue. He had traveled a difficult road to reach the place where his influence would count for something, and he was making genuine progress. Then an amazing picture of betrayal by his closest aides began to unfold. *And a lonely man stood in the shambles of his broken dreams.*

A woman looked back on ten years of happy marriage with the man she loved. She cherished the good life they shared with two beautiful children. Then one day her husband blurted out the unbelievable confession of a sordid affair with a young divorcee. *And a lonely woman wept in the shambles of her broken dreams.*

It is for times like these that the Christian faith was born. The resurrection was not just given to prove immortality. It was an experience of men and women who stood in the dark shadow of a cross on a lonely hill as the symbol of their broken dreams. The resurrection was God's assurance that he would stoop and help them build a new life with their worn-out tools.

Without that confidence, life would be unbearable.